Moving Poetry

Hong Kong Children's Poems

Edited by

Shirley Geok-lin Lim
and
Page Richards

With the assistance of Sonal Srivastava

香港大學出版社
HONG KONG UNIVERSITY PRESS

Hong Kong University Press
14/F Hing Wai Centre
7 Tin Wan Praya Road
Aberdeen
Hong Kong

© Hong Kong University Press 2001

ISBN 962 209 552 6

Secure On-line Ordering
http://www.hkupress.org

Printed and bound by Liang Yu Printing Fty. Ltd., Hong Kong, China.

Contents

Preface

This volume proposes three interrelated goals. The first is to encourage, record, and disseminate the imaginative work of young Hong Kong school children. The second is to produce accompanying materials to the poems that explain the Moving Poetry project in terms of its efficacy for teaching creative and language abilities. The third is to offer strategies for teaching creative writing, particularly poetry, to children in urban, multilingual, and multicultural societies like Hong Kong. However, the constraints of space made it impossible for us to fully engage the last two goals. *Moving Poetry*, in its present form, therefore, serves more as a collection of poems by young Hong Kong children than as a pedagogical textbook for elementary and secondary teachers. The introduction and the afterword do not attempt to develop the materials or to explicate in full the process of teacher training, individual workshop strategies and teacher-student interactions, and relations between the training and strategies and the poems that now appear in this anthology. Rather, we have privileged the poems composed by the children.

We were careful never to write for the children. The young poets possess their own words, images, ideas, and feelings. Revising their drafts, we did note those images that most moved us. We quoted with relish those parts of their language that we found original, pleasing, and surprising; and we suggested revision (and deletion) of excess lines, awkward choices of vocabulary, and infelicities that we recognized from our own poetic practices.

This collection represents only a small percentage of the poems from the workshops. Selection is subjective, perhaps reflecting more of our aesthetic positions and values than the individual poems do. We read all the children's poems. Many lovely ones have not been included. The poet or subject may already have been heavily over-represented, or the poem was too similar in thought or image to another.

We added necessary punctuation. Occasionally, we changed tense endings for subject-verb agreement or consistency. This revising for "proper grammar" was undertaken sparingly; we always wanted to remain faithful to the writer's voice. Our major revision was pruning. A few poems are shorter. We took the responsibility of "editing," that is, dropping weak lines. The majority of poems, though, appear exactly as they were submitted. With two or three, we rearranged the stanzas (not the words). We respected the poems' autonomy. These poems are the poems the children wrote.

Moving Poetry was co-organized by the University of Hong Kong and the Standing Committee on Language Education and Research (SCOLAR), with the support of the Language Fund. We thank the project's Steering Committee and Chairman Mr. Victor Cha, the Department of English at the University of Hong Kong, the university administration, and the University's 90th Anniversary Secretariat for their support of the project. We are grateful to the participating poet-teachers

Louise Ho, Timothy Kaiser, Agnes Lam, Dino Mahoney, Mani Rao, Venus Tsang, Eliza Wong, and Wong Ho-Yin. Our thanks also to the Hong Kong University students who assisted in the workshops: Betty Chan, Sanaz Fotouhi, Cindy Hui, Ruth Hung, Keon Woong Lee, Shalini Nanwani, Carlos C. Perito, Davina To, Nicholas Y.B. Wong and Nicole Wong. Dr. Jennifer McMahon was a superb creative administrator. We also thank the Associate Dean of Education, Dr. K.W. Cheung, who took on the responsibility of outreach to the participating students and schools: Canadian International Primary School; Creative Primary School; Heep Yunn Primary School; Marymount Primary School; Po Leung Kuk Luk Hing Tao Primary School; St. Francis of Assisi's Caritas School; St. Paul's Co-educational [Kennedy Road] Primary School; St. Paul's Co-educational [Macdonnell Road] Primary School; St. Stephen's Girls' Primary School; Victoria English Primary School; Canadian International Secondary School; Law Ting Pong Secondary School; Sacred Heart Canossian College; SKH Bishop Mok Sau Tseng Secondary School; St. Clare's Girls' School; St. Joan of Arc Secondary School; St. Paul's Convent School; True Light Middle School of Hong Kong; and Wah Yan College, Hong Kong. We gratefully salute Pro-Vice-Chancellor Professor K.M. Cheng for sharing our vision. Finally we thank Sonal Srivastava for her help with preparation of the manuscript, the school principals and teachers involved in the project, the parents whose enthusiasm was infectious, and above all the children whose remarkable poems make this anthology possible.

Introduction

What It Takes to Move Poetry: Hong Kong Children's Poems

Shirley Geok-lin Lim

Moving Poetry, celebrating English language school poets from Hong Kong, testifies to our belief in children's amazing creativity and in the joyful work of teaching poetry to young people.

Why should Hong Kong children write poems in English instead of Chinese? The answer is that they should not. Rather, they should feel confident to express themselves in both Chinese and English. As with any poet, they should feel free to write in any language they wish. For a multicultural society like Hong Kong, that language may also be Tagalog, Nepali, Parsi, Hindi, Urdu, Bahasa Indonesian, or any other language spoken as the home language of Hong Kong's many ethnic groups.

The reason why we were focusing our pilot project on poems in English lies partly in Hong Kong's unique history as a Chinese-culture-based British colony. Viewed chiefly as a barren rock in the early nineteenth century, Hong Kong's superb location as a port and gateway for entry into the hinterland of China made it an attractive focus for British colonial expansion in 1841. Pressed by British military victories, China ceded the island to Britain in 1851, and a number of adjacent territories were later added to the colony. Over a hundred years later, on December 19, 1984, China and the United Kingdom signed an agreement for the return of these territories. The handover, recognizing Hong Kong as a Special Administrative Region (SAR) of China under a "one country, two systems" formula, took place on July 1, 1997.

But even before 1997, the role of English in Hong Kong's schools, economy and cultural life had been vigorously debated. Many controversial issues suggested in terms such as bilingualism, cultural nationalism, and mother-tongue education still pertain to post-handover Hong Kong today, just as they have dominated other post-independent discourses in postcolonial countries like Nigeria, Kenya, and, closer home to Hong Kong, Malaysia, the Philippines, and Singapore. Post-1997, it is evident that the century and a half of British rule has left numerous landmarks on Hong Kong's physical and cultural landscape. The place of English as the region's second language is a major legacy that Hong Kong people appear determined to preserve.

This anthology of Hong Kong children's poems in English is particularly timely, coming as it does with the new millennium, a global society connected by the Internet, and English as the language of the new technologies and new economy. At the same time, educational reforms have moved a majority of Hong Kong schools from English to the mother-tongue as the medium of instruction, and anecdotal reports note a diminishing standard of English proficiency throughout the SAR. Economists worry that the decline may contribute to the loss of Hong Kong's competitive edge over other Anglophone-oriented global cities. Indeed, despite the controversies surrounding the role of English in education and in the city's everyday and cultural life, most Hong Kong people agree on the fundamental importance of maintaining English-language standards for Hong Kong in its development as the financial hub of Asia and as Asia's world city. Focusing on children's writing in English, this anthology is also, if only tangentially, responding to and participating in these on-going controversies. The wonderful poems collected here, by the power of the delight they evoke in readers, counter the negative impressions of English-language decline in the SAR.

What has children's poetry to do with momentous political and economic developments? Poets and teachers share a common vision, of the primary significance of intellectual and creative energy to a vital and vibrant community. The future achievements of a great society are potent in our children's imaginations. The English Romantic poet William Blake asked us to see the universe in a grain of sand, and infinity in a flower. How much more can we see in children's capacity for play, surprise, humor, questions, truth-telling, lies — their expressive capabilities in whatever language lies close to their hand! The creative arts, which includes not only literature but also music, drama, painting, and so forth, are central to the new knowledge and cultural industries — so different from the manufacturing base of old Hong Kong — that will lead us in the twenty-first century. Hong Kong's future as a world city thus is integrally related to the way Hong Kong children's imaginative and expressive energies today are released and encouraged.

Moving Poetry offers a selection of poems written by children between the ages of nine and fourteen during workshops taught over three Saturday afternoons, between April 28 to May 12, 2001. Under the rubric of "Moving Poetry," the project brought 160 children from 19 primary and secondary schools to the University of Hong Kong. The children came from a diversity of schools, ranging from international, elite and English Schools Foundation schools to Chinese-language and Band Three (average standard) schools. We were careful to look for gender parity, although generally girls still out-numbered boys, and to include non-elite schools. Working in age-identified groups with international and local teacher-poets, the children received very little instruction on English-language poetic forms and traditions. Instead, they were given models for animal poems, riddle poems, limericks and haiku. They meditated by candle light, listened to music and nature's sounds, talked to each other, and declaimed their poems. Chiefly, they wrote poems and read each others' work.

The Hong Kong Moving Poetry project, as I first conceived it, is not an original concept. In 1972, when I was teaching in New York City, I had read Kenneth Koch's seminal book, *Wishes, Lies and Dreams*, which offered the first notable introduction to teaching children to write poetry. Koch wanted not only to expose children to poetry but also to help young children to write their own poetry through classes taught by visiting practicing poets. Learning from students and teachers, Koch began to publish his ideas and students' poems in a variety of places. *Wishes, Lies and Dreams* became a classic, still in print after almost 30 years. Koch's project, supported by the non-profit group Teachers & Writers Collaborative, is now reproduced in various forms throughout the United States, thus in 1997, I taught school children as young as eight in Patterson, New Jersey as part of the Poets-in-the-Schools program. This anthology owes much of its spirit of play, improvisation, experimentation, openness and, in homage, even a chapter heading to Koch's personal account of the strategies, assignments, ideas, and successes in his classes.

Convinced that Hong Kong children's imagination can be nurtured in English, I first had to identify poet-teachers willing to take on the challenge. Those who agreed to work on the project have all published in smaller or greater degree. More, we all agree on the fundamental importance of the written word, on the central significance of beauty indivisible in form, thought, and feeling. We spent one afternoon discussing Koch's ideas and modifications of them, as well as original approaches that would work best for local children. We arrived at some collective strategies, but each of us also adopted some individual approaches. For example, concerned that the primary school children might feel alienated or fearful at finding themselves in the imposing classrooms of the university's near-century-old Main Building, I suggested that the children be welcomed to their first workshop with a present of a toy animal. Clutching their stuffed bear, unicorn, rabbit or snake, the children in my workshop read William Blake's "Tyger,

Tyger, Burning Bright" as a model for their own animal poem. This early exercise encouraged them to understand the effectiveness of repetition as a principle of form, music and intensity, as well as the primary significance of a dominant image and an appeal to the senses.

In other workshops, teachers used candles whose light in a darkened room served to help the children relax and call up memories, images and fantasies. Others deployed CDs of nature sounds to encourage concentration and meditation. Certain subjects also proved highly effective in evoking images; writing about favorite foods, for instance, led to strong, culturally-specific poems even from children as young as eleven. Agnes Lam provided her primary school children with selected structures. For example, she asked them to think about what they would do when they grew up, and to write these ideas as "When I____, I ____." She gave them postcards on Hong Kong and asked them to write about their experience of places, things or people in Hong Kong.

With the secondary school children, Dino Mahoney used the well-known nursery rhyme "What are little boys made of? What are little girls made of?" to provoke a series of wonderfully sharp, irreverent, comic, and memorable poems. Mani Rao, also working with teenagers, wrote, "Our subjects evolved with the sessions. I began with the very objective 'Why do I like trees' to warm up and moved on to a fantastic topic 'A journey to the moon.' In the second and third sessions we were able to tackle the more personal 'What I want to be,' and the group poems about colours." Louise Ho, who worked with the oldest group of teenagers, began with a free writing exercise to contrast a minimum use of control over language with a maximum control over language usage, and to emphasize that poetry is language at its most precise and concise. Exercises in rhythm provided her students with an initial sense of poetry as technique and training. In contrast, Wong Ho Yin encouraged his secondary school students to write on "weird things." In reading their "Wish" poems, he asked students to work in small groups to select one line each that they regarded as the craziest. Those lines were then collected and rendered into a class poem.

The Moving Poetry project thus brought eager children together with poets who knew how to stimulate and encourage play in the life-affirming genre of poetry. This collection records the success of the workshops; the poems written during those Saturday afternoons have been edited with chiefly a popular and secondarily an academic audience in mind. Appearing in the same year as and dedicated to the 90th anniversary of the University of Hong Kong, the anthology reminds us of the significance of the English language in Hong Kong's cultural history and contemporary life. The University of Hong Kong, the oldest university in Hong Kong, first established in 1911, possesses a particularly distinguished record in English higher education and continues to maintain its role as the premier English-language university in Hong Kong and China. The support for the workshops in fact came from a centrally administered project to help grow a creative English writing culture in Hong Kong schools and in Hong Kong society as a whole.

Moving Poetry is the first publication coming out of Hong Kong, and indeed out of the Southeast Asian region, that takes children's voices seriously. It is no exaggeration to describe their poems as possessing imaginative power. The anthology therefore occupies a pioneering position in the history of English-language, pedagogical, and literary publications in the SAR. We are looking forward to future collections, so that this book will not long remain the only one of its kind. Indeed, it is my hope that the anthology augers a series of anthologies, with two or three appearing over the course of ten years, and with a Hong Kong University 100th anniversary commemorative volume appearing in 2011.

But perhaps that is to look too far into the future. What these children's poems show us, instead, is that the present tense of the imagination vibrates within the confines of the shapes of their poems. Our pleasure in their words, thoughts, and feelings is the pleasure universally shared through surprising resemblance and original discovery, through seeing infinity in the grain of childhood.

Food

and

Animals

Moving Poetry

The Sweet

The first time I ate sweets,
It was a strawberry sweet.
Oh! It was so sour.
Tooooooooo! I spat it out.
After that I didn't like strawberries anymore.

And I tried to eat grape sweets.
Em . . . . . it tasted toooooo sweet,
So I don't like grapes anymore.

After 1997,
I have found a Green Tea Sweet
At a Japanese Restaurant.
It suits me!
It is not too sweet or too sour.
It's just right.

Zoe Lavinia Lau
Primary 5, St. Stephen's Girls' Primary School

The goose eats seafood,
as it chases small fishes
in the ocean.

Honk Honk Gulp.

Justin Ho
Primary 5, St. Paul's Co-Ed (Macdonnell Road) Primary School

My Whale Speaks of Gibberish

I've known gibberish.
I've known gibberish, as nonsensical as Xavier.

My spirit has grown like the giberman's.

I learned giberphibit very hard.
I drank the purest water from gibberzon.

Philip Lui
Primary 5, Canadian International School

Rice Dumpling

I'm Miss Rice Dumpling.
I'm made of rice and pork.
I smell nice and soft.

I'm Mr. Rice Dumpling.
My clothes are green and
My inside is light brown.
And I am salty.
If you eat me too much
You will be sick.

Ching Yi
Primary 6, PLK Luk Hing Too Primary School

The Beauty of a Fish

In the gleaming stream under the glow of the sun,
I saw a goldfish
On the curve of the water's body
Dancing like a ballet dancer
Spinning among the blossoming flowers
To the flapping sound of the fish's fin slapping the
    stream.

Melanie Hau
Primary 5, St. Stephen's Girls' Primary School

My rabbit nibbles everything
in a big cupboard —

mm mm the sound is
softer than someone whispering —

pausing to take some breaths,
being squashed like a mashed
potato.

Tavis Jason Liu
Primary 5, St. Paul's Co-Ed (Macdonnell Road) Primary School

The rooster gobbles up corn
munching and munching, its teeth
sogging into the delicious inner of the corn, leaving
    yellow
stains on its teeth —

crunch, crunch, creating a lovely
jazz band harmony, pausing minute after minute

to breathe.
Every piece of corn presents a musical
instrument of the group.

Andrea Lee
Primary 5, St. Paul's Co-Ed (Kennedy Road) Primary School

Pasta

I am a tasty pasta.
I wear a red dress with ribbons.
I look like thousands of snails.
But the children love me.
Yesterday I was straight and clean.
But I played with the tomato sauce.
I went red and red and red.
Someone pushed me into a wok.
I went hotter, hotter . . .
Afterwards, I slept in a white bowl.
Then I was gone,
Gone into somebody's mouth.

Tiffany Lee
Primary 6, Heep Yunn Primary School

Moving Poetry

The Sting Ray

Meeting him in the sunken castle
Of the ocean bed,
His tail is like a screw,
His eyes are like small balls,
His mouth is like a banana,
His wings are like carpets.

But his brain is a green water balloon.

Derek Kam
Primary 5, St. Paul's Co-Ed (Macdonnell Road) Primary School

My Trip to My Panda

Meeting her in the forest
It seems a forest of light.
Her nose is like a triangle,
Her face is like a furry softball,
Her bow-tie is like a shining tomato,
Her hidden nails are like fish scales,
Her eyes are like two meatballs.

But her soul is a bright sun.

Annie Bu
Primary 5, Victoria English Primary School

The Seal

Meeting him in the Atlantic Ocean,
It seems an ocean of cold icebergs.
His tail is like coral.
His fin is like a seagull's wing.
His whiskers are like an old man's beard.
His eyes are like stars glowing in the dark.
His back is like a rainbow above the sea.

But his heart is like the dark cold mysterious ocean.

Melanie Hau
Primary 5, St. Stephen's Girls' Primary School

The Donkey Munches Berries

Yum, yum, yum, the donkey picks
berries. Some sweet and juicy,
good! Sour sour and dry, ew!

Makes a munching-choir, pausing
to listen to the sound of the juicy berries.

Stephanie Tsang
Primary 5, St. Stephen's Girls' Primary School

Carrot Cake

Coming out from the kitchen
Is an enormous carrot cake
With a strong carrot smell and yummy dressing
Which makes my mouth water!
I like it and so does Grandmother.
It's the only thing we like together.

Karine Chan
Primary 6, Heep Yunn Primary School

Chicken Feet

Chicken feet! Smell it!
Its smell is flying towards the sky.
People around the world smell it,
And they all fall in love with it.

Chicken feet! Coming!
It is sitting on its lovely plate.
All other dim sum lose their shine.
Soon it will be eaten completely.

Law Kar Yee
Primary 6, Heep Yunn Primary School

The Shark

Shark! Shark! Rainy wet,
In a forest when it thunders,
What's your body when it's wet?
Can you make it clean?

Chau Ton
Primary 6, PLK Luk Hing Too Primary School

The Bear Falls Asleep

The bear falls gently on
the moist grass, its eyes
closing.

A gentle rumbling escapes
from its nose
as it is pulled into
a vortex of food, colors and dreams.

Eugenia Ng
Primary 6, Canadian International School

The Diving Goose

Among the creatures of the deep,
I saw a goose,
in metallic grey,
diving in the abyss,
stealthily, neck straight.

Ho Ching, Justin
Primary 5, St. Paul's Co-Ed (Macdonnell Road) Primary School

The Puppy

Meeting him in the cage at my home,
It seems a huge camera.
His tail is like a colourful straw
His ears are like pieces of cheese
His paws are like two soft pillows
His spots are like dirt on a piece of white cloth
His eyes are like seeds of an orange
But his heart is a big, red peach.

Lee Ka Chun, Kevin
Primary 5, St. Paul's Co-Ed (Macdonnell Road) Primary School

Taro Cake

Taro cake is big and square.
Its taste is salty like soya sauce.
On Sundays at my kind grandma's house,
I make a sound eating: hmm!

Jennifer Chow
Primary 6, Marymount Primary School

Shrimp Dumplings

Hmm, yum, a warm shrimp dumpling on my tongue.
So rubbery, crunchy. That really pleases me.
Go to a Chinese restaurant and you'll hear,
Squash, squash, everyone's munching.

Michelle Lee
Primary 6, Marymount Primary School

Bear! Bear! Shouting loud
In the forests of the noon,
What happened to you?
Could you stop shouting?

Mo Chun Kit
Primary 6, PLK Luk Hing Too Primary School

The Lion

Lion, lion, you bark loud
So everyone's afraid of you.
People think you're dangerous,
But I think you're kind.

When everyone sees you
You're barking loudly.
But when I see you
You're singing sweetly.

Sharon Tang
Primary 6, Heep Yunn Primary School

Rabbit

Meeting him in the forest
he seems a big white carrot.
His tail is like a snowball.
His eyes are like small black apples.
His nose is like a hard peach.
His whiskers are like pink soft branches.
But his heart is playful.

Tavis Jason Liu
Primary 5, St. Paul's Co-Ed (Macdonnell Road) Primary School

The Snake

The handsome and spotty old snake was jogging
on the road towards the grass. In the hot sun,
his hands and legs were thin but strong,
and two logs were along the road.

Matthew Wong
Primary 5, St. Paul's Co-Ed (Kennedy Road) Primary School

My Seal Speaks of the Sun

I've known the sun.
I've known the sun warm like family and bright like
   the moon.

I've crawled lazily under the sun.
I fell asleep in the sunny day.
I thought of gliding above the sun.
I've always lived under the sun.

I've known the sun until a grey cloud takes its place.

Melanie Hau
Primary 5, St. Stephen's Girls' Primary School

Grape

Looks like the earth.
Colors the ink of my pen.
Smells like a mango.
Sweet taste.
Feels like rubber.

Jessica Sze
Form 1, St. Clare's Girls' School

Lemon

Looks like cat's eyes
Smells like spoiled milk
Feels like a golf ball
Looks like a sliced up wheel.

Jenny Cheng
Form 2, Sacred Heart Canossian College

Pony

I am a pony, a browny coated little pony.
I have a shining coat that shines in the sunlight.
I like to run in the morning in the field.
While everyone still sleeps,
I like to run, run and run.
You can see me in the mountains and up the hills.
If you see me, don't be afraid. But don't forget to feed
    me.
I am a pony, a browny coated little pony.
Run, run and run like the wind.
I feel proud of my beautiful coat.
I won't be ashamed when you see me.
Come to see me now.
If you hear me, neigh, neigh.
You know I am trotting by
like the wind, the wind.

June Lau
Primary 6, Heep Yunn Primary School

My Cat Lee

I have a cat
Called Amy.
She likes to go
Into the kitchen
Step by step.
When I see
Her there,
She runs away.

Ka Yee, Kiki
Primary 6, St. Francis of Assisi's Caritas School

The Skunk

Meeting him on the court,
It seems a rainbow of colors.
His tail is like the wings of birds.
His ears are like candy made of cotton.
His paws are like bananas hanging on the tree.
His stripes are like lines on the court.

But his heart is a basketball that is dribbled
    by a player left and right.

Xavier Tam
Primary 6, Canadian International School

Chinchilla

Proud of my dark sparkling eyes,
Proud of my plain soothing fur,
Proud of my special name,
Proud of my pure thinking.
But deep in my heart,
Smolder flames of hate
For greedy hunters
Who steal our fur.
Run, run, they come to destroy our homes!
Run, run, they come to take our furs!
Those unforgivable humans.
Chit-Chit.

Michelle Lee
Primary 6, Marymount Primary School

Pineapple

Hard and dry outside,
Green hat on head,
Painful to touch you,
But sweet to taste you –
That's why I like you.

Strong and well-built,
Look at you.
In a desert,
I cut you,
Like a cactus.

Anita Mak
Form 2, Sacred Heart Canossian College

Wishes, Lies,

and

Riddles

I wish I were a wise wizard
I wish I had a waggery wand
I wish it had weird wonders
I wish my wonders were as wild as the north wind
I wish the north wind would not whisper like worms
I wish the worms would not wiggle into my walls.

Angela Cheung
Primary 5, Marymount Primary School

Wishes

I wish I had an elder sister, as kind as a fairy
    godmother.
I wish I owned a black limousine, as long as the
    Amazon River.
I wish I were an old oak tree, with birds perching on
    me.
I wish I lived in a volcano, with red and orange
    everywhere.
I wish I were an alien, with branches on my head.
I wish I were a Porsche, driven by men really fast.
I wish I were a blackboard, with words written on me.
I wish my father were a woman, so he won't be so
    fierce.
I wish my school were built in space, so I could go to
    school on UFOs.
I wish Hong Kong was a green city, with fresh air and
    a nice environment.

Jeannette Ip
Primary 6, Marymount Primary School

Riddle Poem

When it's very cold,
I'm very hard.
When the weather is mild,
I move about wherever I like.
When it gets very hot,
I fly with the wind.

(answer: water)

Candy Chan
Form 3, True Light Middle School

I wish I can go to America.
I wish I can go to Neverland with Peter Pan.
I wish my home can be as big as the sky.
I wish I have pink wings and can play on the moon.
I wish I can eat a bowl of ice-cream everyday.

Cossette Lau
Primary 6, PLK Luk Hing Too Primary School

I Wish

I wish I could be wind.
I wish I could be a wind designer.
I wish I could be a wind designer as I could blow the
Cold wind through the window.

Tsang Hei Man
Primary 6, St. Francis of Assisi's Caritas School

Riddle Poem

You like to eat my fins,
I like to eat you.

(answer: a shark)

Derek Chan
Form 2, Wah Yan College

I wish I can fly on the magic mat with Aladdin.
I wish I can live in ancient China.
I wish I can have a free ride on a dinosaur.
I wish I can make friends with children all over the
world.

Karine Chan
Primary 6, Heep Yunn Primary School

I wish I were as powerful as a genie, to fill my life
    with colors.
I wish to have a jester at home, to make me happy
    all day.
I wish to live in a sea castle, with the mermaids.
I wish to have ten more wishes.

Michelle Li
Primary 5, Marymount Primary School

Riddle Poem

If my brother is lost
Then I'm no use.

(answer: chopsticks)

Wong Wing Tat
Form 2, Wah Yan College

I wish I can have ten million dollars to buy an old
    expensive violin.
I wish I can live under the sea so I can play with the
    fish.
I wish I can be the sky, so that I can look far around
    the world.

Sharon Tang
Primary 6, Heep Yunn Primary School

Wishes

I wish I can travel around the world in 80 days.
I wish I can meet God and ask him to give me his
    telephone number.
I wish I can have three legs, so I can run faster.
I wish I can buy a brand new CD and listen to it until
    I go deaf.
I wish I can lie on a beach and let mosquitoes fly
    around me.
I wish I can be a turtle and just sleep in my home all
    day.
I wish I can live in the South Pole and feed the
    penguins.
I wish to be the color light blue and cover the sky.

Katherine Law
Primary 6, Heep Yunn Primary School

Big Lie Poem

Madonna asked me to adopt her,
But I declined.
I live in the red of a rainbow
And have a cloud for a pet.
I walk with my eyes
And see with my feet.
I invented the light bulb,
But nobody noticed.

Carol Yu
Form 3, Canadian International School

Wishes

I wish my friend, Tom, can be more happy.
I wish I can fly, that I can travel around the world.
I wish I can be a tiger, then I can run very fast and
    eat other animals.
I wish I have a city called Sam City, then I can do
    anything in this city.
I wish I can be time, then I can make time fast, or
    make time slow.

Mo Chun Kit, Sam
Primary 6, PLK Luk Hing Too Primary School

Big Lie Poem

I am Bill Gates and
I come from Pluto.
I am twelve feet tall
And I see with my ears
And hear with my eyes.
Last week I played mahjong with Napoleon.

Lai King Lok
Form 2, Wah Yan College

Riddle Poem

I'm strange.
When people hit me,
I come alive,
But when people don't hit me,
I get upset
And stay silent.

(answer: a drum)

Candy Chan
Form 3, True Light Middle School

I wish I were rich.
No, that doesn't matter.

I wish I had magical powers.
No, something better.

I want to wish for many things
Whatever they may be.

But all I really wish is
to be me.

Coco Marett
Form 1, Canadian International School

Riddle Poem

I am obedient,
Loyal to my master.
Often hidden, I am shy,
But I like showing off in a spotlight.

(answer: a shadow)

Carol Yu
Form 3, Canadian International School

Riddle Poem

I have three hands,
They are all runners.
They never stop running
But they run at different speeds.
One can run twenty four laps a day.

(answer: a clock)

Keith Cheng
Form 2, Wah Yan College

I wish I were a bird flying in the sky.
I wish I were a flower enjoying sunshine.
I wish I were a star watching the city from the sky.
I wish I were a person living without worry.
I wish I were an airplane, which can travel anywhere.
I wish I were a map holding the ocean and land.

Jenny Cheng
Form 2, Sacred Heart Canossian College

Limericks
and
Haiku

Snow

Ah! Snow is quite white.
It drops on the blue sea
Like a white paper.

Jennifer Chow
Primary 6, Marymount Primary School

There was a young man from Shek O
Who hated to play the piano.
He hated to play
And he hated to stay
So he hurried away from Shek O.

Melissa Yeung
Form 2, True Light Middle School

Loneliness
is a friend
of the elderly.

Chu Christy
Form 2, True Light Middle School

There was an old man of Sheung Wan
Who lived in a rusty tin can
And this can had got stuck
In the back of a truck
Which was hurtling out of Sheung Wan.

Serena Wong
Form 2, True Light Middle School

Mooncake

Who bakes a mooncake
During the Chinese New Year
With some chocolate?

Wong Wing Na, Irene
Form 2, SKH Bishop Mok Sau Tseng Secondary School

I look at the bird,
The bird looks at me.
Where's the exit? Where's the exit?

Serena Wong
Form 2, True Light Middle School

There was a young boy of Tun Mun,
Who liked to look up at the moon.
When he moved to Shatin
It grew very dim
So he took a bus back to Tun Mun.

Keith Cheng
Form 2, Wah Yan College

A cockroach has eight legs
But it runs slower than
A rat with four legs.

Ko Chi Ching
Form 2, Wah Yan College

There was a young man of Tun Mun
Who wanted to fly to the moon.
So he jumped on a bottle
And called it a shuttle,
That clever young man of Tun Mun.

Ko Chi Ching
Form 2, Wah Yan College

A greedy mouse
Happily eating the cheese
Without thinking it's a trap.

Cheung Ka Yu
Form 2, Wah Yan College

There was a young boy from Wanchai
Whose Mum was a secret firefly
And now every night
He burns very bright
That amazing young boy from Wanchai.

Lai King Lok
Form 2, Wah Yan College

A fan is turning
My head is spinning
On a hot summer night.

Josephine Wong
Form 2, True Light Middle School

There was a young man from Shek O
Who liked watching the sea and the snow.
Once he saw a tsunami
And cried out, 'Oh Mummy!'
That curious young man from Shek O.

Christy Chu
Form 2, True Light Middle School

Ants are very hardworking
So why do people
Like killing them?

Cheung Ka Yu
Form 2, Wah Yan College

There was an old man of Sheung Wan,
Whose best friend was called Mister Kwan.
They both taught applied science
With enormous defiance,
Those exhilarating old men of Sheung Wan.

Christy Chu
Form 2, True Light Middle School

Small bird in a cage
looks to the sky
with hopeless eyes

Bryan Lie
Form 2, Wah Yan College

Bathtub

Filled to the brim,
a bowl of pure joy
releases the stress.

Michael Paskewitz
Form 2, Canadian International School

I sit here
Watching a butterfly
Flying further and further away

Josephine Wong
Form 2, True Light Middle School

A paper fan.
A beautiful woman hides behind it
While lots of men peep at her.

Christy Chu
Form 2, True Light Middle School

A cat jumps over
My tiny scared heart –
And stops.

Chan Chun Ho, Derek
Form 2, Wah Yan College

There was an old lady of Jordan
Who lived all her life as an orphan.
She sold smelly fish
And was very selfish,
That greedy old lady of Jordan.

Dorothy Chan
Form 3, Law Ting Pong Secondary School

There was a young lady of Lamma
Whose husband was a drunken old farmer.
So she filled him with wine
Until he felt fine,
That clever young lady of Lamma.

Dorothy Chan
Form 3, Law Ting Pong Secondary School

So many people
so much noise
and only me.

Jeffrey Au
Form 3, Canadian International School

There was a young lady of Lamma
Who was soon to become a young mamma.
But her mother said 'no!'
So she soon had to go
Out of boring, old-fashioned old Lamma.

Jeffery Au
Form 3, Canadian International School

Pen Twiddle Disease

My friends twiddle their pens.
I used to get annoyed with them,
But now I twiddle too.

Karen Ho
Form 3, St. Paul's Convent School

There was a young boy of Tun Mun
Who had, for a pet, a baboon
That ate chili pepper
And ran from a leper,
That crazy young boy from Tun Mun.

Jeffery Au
Form 3, Canadian International School

I need a saw
To break out from this cage
And fly away with the wind.

Candy Chan
Form 3, Law Ting Pong Secondary School

There was a young lady of Lamma
Who was not very good at her grammar.
Her words none understood,
Not even the smartest could,
That crazy young lady of Lamma.

Carol Yu
Form 3, Canadian International School

Little Girls,

Little Boys,

and

Lazy Persons

What Are Little Girls Made Of?

What are little girls made of, made of?
Lace dresses and the wind of spring,
Sweet kisses flying through the air,
A juicy peach hanging from a tree
With lots of butterflies flying around it.
A piano playing automatic love songs.

What are little boys made of, made of?
Animal waste and methane gas,
Cockroach legs and CFC,
Rows of shark teeth
And a tongue made of a bloody knife.

Christy Chu
Form 2, True Light Middle School

Lazy Teacher's Song

I could have a better career, but I'm too lazy to look
for one.
There are a lot of students in my class, but I'm too
lazy to teach them.
There are lots of test papers, but I'm too lazy to mark
them.
So they pile up in walls around my desk.
There are lots of meetings, but I'm too lazy to attend.
So the principal is going to fire me,
But I'm too lazy to care.
There's a benchmark test for teachers, but I'm too
lazy to study for it,
And even if I did study, I'd be too lazy to walk to the
exam hall.
There are lessons to prepare, but I'm too lazy to
open the books.
People say that students in Hong Kong are lazy,
But even they are not as lazy as I.

Josephine Wong
Form 2, True Light Middle School

What Are Little Girls Made Of?

What are little girls made of, made of?
Mozart's music and juicy peaches,
Mona Lisa's smile and Julia Robert's grin.

What are little boys made of, made of?
Stale beef and pork and rusted metal,
Ammonia, barbarian blood and fleas.

Melissa Yeung
Form 2, True Light Middle School

Lazy Mother's Song

I have a family, but I'm too lazy to love them.
I have a flat, but I'm too lazy to clean it.
My son is crying, but I'm too lazy to hug him.
My daughter is smiling, but I'm too lazy to smile with
    her.
When I am happy, I am too lazy to laugh,
When sad, too lazy to cry.
I want to feed my family, but I'm too lazy to cook.
My husband loves me, but I'm too lazy to love him
    back.
My husband yells at me, but I'm too lazy to yell back.
My mother used to boast that she was lazy,
But she used to cook and wash the clothes,
So even she was not as lazy as I.

Candy Chan
Form 3, Law Ting Pong Secondary School

What Are Little Boys Made Of?

What are little boys made of, made of?
School songs, pens and money,
Energy, sunlight and space,
Rocks, stones and sand.

What are little girls made of, made of?
Sadness and loneliness,
Pork chops and broken clothes,
Durian rind and broken finger nails.

Derek Chan
Form 2, Wah Yan College

The Lazy Father's Song

I could have a job, but I'm too lazy to find one.
I have children, but I'm too lazy to teach them
So they now they are just as naughty as wild
    monkeys.
I have a flute, but I'm too lazy to play,
So my flute might as well be a piece of rusted iron.
The kitchen chair is broken, but I'm too lazy to mend
    it.
My wife tells me there is no free lunch.
I want to work, but I'm too lazy to go for an interview.
My son and daughter love me and I should love them
    too,
But I'm just too lazy to love people.

Dorothy Chan
Form 3, Law Ting Pong Secondary School

What Are Little Boys Made Of?

What are little boys made of, made of?
Muscles and dragons and bricks and birds,
Sea and sky and music and love,
Ducks, cartoons, and wisdom and brains.

What are little girls made of, made of?
Pork chops and mice and nonsense and exams,
Destruction and caterpillars, wasps and bees,
Nonsense and monsters and darkness and sin.

Bryan Lie
Form 2, Wah Yan College

Lazy Father's Song

I've got a job, but I'm too lazy to go to it.
I've got money, but I'm too lazy to spend it
So it's just the same as if I had no money.
I'm sleepy, but I'm too lazy to go to bed.
I have children, but I'm too lazy to spend time with
    them.
When they are naughty, I'm too lazy to spank them.
I'm in debt, but I'm too lazy to pay back the money.
I like to gamble, but I'm too lazy to go to a casino.
My wife tells me to treat her better.
I want to give her gifts, but I'm too lazy to buy them.
You may think you are lazier than me,
But even you took the time to read this poem.

Jeffery Au
Form 3, Canadian International School

What Are Little Girls Made Of, Made Of?

What are little girls made of, made of?
Snakes and rubbish and SO_2,
Rust and toothpaste and rotten apples.

What are little boys made of, made of?
Laughter and singing and music,
Cleverness, gold and long summer days,
Sport, happiness, angels and a pure cup of H_2O.

Jimmy Ko
Form 2, Wah Yan College

What Are Little Girls Made Of?

What are little girls made of, made of?
Old food stuck between the teeth
And the noses of pigs,
Snake hearts
And witches' brooms.

What are little boys made of, made of?
Beethoven symphonies,
Angel wings,
Bright sunshine

And rainbows.

Lai King Lok
Form 2, Wah Yan College

I could have a school uniform,
but I am too lazy to choose one that fits.
I have bought the text books,
but I am too lazy to bring them to school.
My black shoes have a big hole,
but I am too lazy to repair them.
My homework is wrong, but I am too lazy to correct it.
I have my own locker, but I am too lazy to put the
    books into it,
so it's just the same as if my locker is full of dust.
I have got friends, but I am too lazy to talk,
so it's just the same as if I have no friends.
Other students invite me to cheat in the exam.
I want to get high marks, but I am too lazy to cheat.
I have always been told that Peter
passes his whole life in absolute idleness.
But he brings his text books and sometimes cheats,
so even he is not as lazy as I.

Cheung Ka Yu
Form 2, Wah Yan College

What Are Little Boys Made Of?

What are little boys made of, made of?
Animal waste and sago worms,
With the brains of a dinosaur
And the heart of a wolf.

What are little girls made of, made of?
Rainbows and the smell of flowers,
Butterflies, birdsong
And cold ice cream.

Josephine Wong
Form 2, True Light Middle School

What Are Little Girls Made Of?

What are little girls made of, made of?
Sewer slime and dirty nails,
Morning breath and nails scratching on a blackboard,
Zits and skunk tails
And thick boring novels and cat droppings.

What are little boys made of, made of?
A good night's sleep and a beautiful sunrise.
Respect and pride.
Triple plays and loads of 3-pointers,
Shark's fin soup and ice cream floats.

Jeffery Au
Form 3, Canadian International School

What Are Pretty Girls Made Of?

What are pretty girls made of, made of?
Vitamin A
Vitamin C
Vitamin D
And vitamin E.
Protein,
Dietary fibre,
Simple distillation
And happy flirtation.

Candy Chan
Form 3, True Light Middle School

What Are Little Boys Made Of?

What are little boys made of, made of?
Pleasure, glory and angel wings,
Tenderness, metal and warm water,
Dictionaries, brains and rubber bands.

What are little girls made of, made of?
Nonsense, animal dung and broken clothes,
Darkness, dustbins and dirty words,
Nonsense, hamburgers and baby machines.

Andrew Leung
Form 2, Wah Yan College

Candles

and

Other Matters

When I Am Happy

When I am happy,
I jump up.

When I am sad,
I drink 7-up.

When I am angry,
I eat a Chupa-Chup.

When I am lonely,
I throw some plastic cups.

Chris Tsui
Primary 4, Victoria English Primary School

When I Grow Up

When I grow up,
I want to be an artist.

I'll draw my future.
I'll draw my past.
I'll draw my happiness.
I'll draw my sadness.

Angela Li
Primary 4, Marymount Primary School

People Who Live in Hong Kong

People who live in Hong Kong
are very busy.
Every day they go to work,
work and work.
Why don't they play or sleep?

People who live in Hong Kong
go to work by the MTR.
They are all tired and sit quietly.
I think they didn't have
a good sleep last night.

Women who live in Hong Kong
always play with one another.
But sometimes they don't cook dinner.
Why? Because they all have a servant.

People who live in Hong Kong
are all very busy.

Helen Lai
Primary 4, St. Paul's Co-Ed (Kennedy Rd) Primary School

Digger Tells Me

Digger tells me
he is poor.
He has no sister,
no little brother.

Digger tells me
he doesn't like my bed.
He always sleeps in
my dirty old clothes.

He does not know
how good my bed is.
He does not know
how bad my clothes are!

Helen Lai
Primary 4, St. Paul's Co-Ed (Kennedy Rd) Primary School

My shoes are as shiny as fireflies at night.
My anger is as rosy as popping lava.
My father's kindness is as delicate as rare scallops.
My mom's mind is as focused as worker bees.
My granny's heart is as nice as melting brown cube
    sugars.

Kelly Wei
Primary 5, Marymount Primary School

Colour

Red is hot lava pouring from a volcano.
Blue is the ocean stretching to the edge of azure.
Green is the evergreen tree throughout the seasons.
White is the daytime as bright as a star.

Brennan Leung
Primary 5, Canadian International School

The Rugby Ball

Among the grassy fields
I saw a rugby ball
in my hand
running
through the other players,
the crowd cheering
with their hands.

Tavis Jason Liu
Primary 5, St. Paul's Co-Ed (Macdonnell Road) Primary School

I used to be a goldfish
But now I am a black toad.
I used to be a red flower
But now I am brown earth.
I used to be a bridge
But now I am a river.
I used to be a rainbow
But now I am a dark cloud.
I used to be the sun
But now I am a broken lamp.

Mina Ip
Primary 5, Creative Primary School

Candle

A little match, same as the sun.
Becomes hot and hot,
Gets bright and bright.

A little match, same as a baby.
Crying loud and loud,
Feeling hungry and hungry.

A little match, same as an apple.
Tastes sweet and sweet,
Eating much and much.

Eunice Chung
Primary 6, PLK Luk Hing Too Primary School

My School

The school bell goes ling a ling a ling
And there is a moment of
Silence.
A teacher is talking about the prayers.
A boy is laughing haha.
All students are going back tip tap tip tap
To have their lessons.
The bells goes
Ling a ling a ling
And the lessons end.

Mae Tsung Sin, Mei
Primary 6, St. Francis of Assisi's Caritas School

Under My Bed

Every night I hear knock knock
Under my bed.
I want to see what is there,
But I am afraid.
Is there a ghost,
A mouse
Or a dog?
There is another world
With many secrets.

Lau Ho Bong, Howard
Primary 6, Victoria English Primary School

Moon

I can see
A red moon
In the morning.
And I can see
A black moon
at midnight.
Why do I say that?
Because I'm dreaming now.

Lee Ka Yee, Kiki
Primary 6, St. Francis of Assisi's Caritas School

Red

The sun is red but
I think it is black.
The lemon is yellow but
I think it is black.
Why do I say that?
Because I am unhappy now.

Lung Pui Shan, Cecilia
Primary 6, St. Francis of Assisi's Caritas School

An angry teacher.
Her face is like a lion.
My chair goes backwards.
She roars, a mad lion.

Jennifer Chow
Primary 6, Marymount Primary School

Meeting him in a disco,
It seems a disco of bad, bad bears.

His eyes are like disco balls.
His nose is like a piece of ice in a cocktail cup.
His armpit is like an unrolled cigarette.
His earring is like the earring of a teenage boy.
His neck is like the neck of a wine bottle.

But his liver is an alcohol-burning machine.

Philip Lui
Primary 6, Canadian International School

My Baby Brother

My baby brother has the material look of a Chinese
    doll
With big eyes.
From them spirits glow.
They look like caves in that sweet face.
His hands feel like paste,
Smooth and oily, snowy like milk.

Yu Sze Wing, Bianca
Primary 6, St. Stephen's Girls' Primary School

Last Time and This Time

When I was three I could walk.
Now I can run very fast.
When I was three I couldn't swim.
Now I can swim, but very slow.
When I was three I played with water.
Now I play with my computer.
When I was three I was bitten by my dog.
Now I hit my dog.
When I was three I was afraid of rats.
Now I have a fat cat.

Mo Chun Kit, Sam
Primary 6, PLK Luk Hing Too Primary School

Feeling

If you are asking whether I am lonely,
well, yes, I am lonely,
like a cactus standing miserable in the desert,
with no friends, for everyone's afraid of my needles.
If you are asking whether I am lonely,
well, yes, I am lonely,
like the lonely moon in the velvet sky,
for sure there is only one moon.
If you are asking whether I am lonely,
well, yes, I am lonely,
like a lemon in the big metal fruit plate,
for people never eat me.
I am only the background for other fruits,
they only want me for my color.

Michelle Lee
Primary 6, Marymount Primary School

I used to be a red apple, but now I am a brown apple
   pie.
I used to be a stone, but now I am a diamond.

I used to be a greedy billionaire, but now I am a
   greedy beggar.
I used to work hard, but now I am extremely lazy.

Once I was a clean forest but now I am a dirty city.
Once I was a green tree but now I am a piece of
   white paper.
Once the dog was barking but now it is dying.

Once I was a student but now I am a librarian.
Once my grandpa was a young man but now he has
   no hair on his head.
I used to be a man, but now I am a skeleton.

Katherine Law
Primary 6, Heep Yunn Primary School

Feeling

If you are asking whether I am tired,
well, yes, I am tired like a car being driven from
China to Egypt for days and days, months and
months, years and years without stopping.
Of course I am tired, like a bull brought to the
amphitheatre in Rome for bull-baiting for the
whole day.
If you want to know if I am tired, I am tired, like an
old grandfather clock, tick-tocking 24 hours non-
stop, but without getting anyone's attention.

Jeanette Ip
Primary 6, Marymount Primary School

Feeling

If you are asking whether I am sad, yes, I am sad like
a parrot
trapped by hunger. It will die anyhow because of the
pollution that people produce.
Of course I am sad, like a dolphin caught by four
fishermen and slowly dying in water polluted by
factories.
You want to know if I am sad. I am sad, like a dog
whose owner always turns on the television at
night and plays the drums so loudly that they
break my ears.

Jennifer Chow
Primary 6, Marymount Primary School

Last Time and This Time

Once I was a cloud, but now I am a raindrop.
Once I was lady, but now I am a ghost.
Once I was a seedling, but now I am a big tree.
Once I was a tree, but now I am a piece of paper.
Once I was snow, but now I am a snowman.
Once I was a train so I run very fast, but now I am a
    tram so I run very slow.
Once I was cloth, but now I am a beautiful dress.
Once I was metal, but now I am metal ware.
Once I was an English Colony, but now I am a
    Chinese state.

Chan So Man, Amy
Primary 6, PLK Luk Hing Too Primary School

Feeling

If you are asking whether I am worried,
Well, yes. I am worried like a P.6 student who is
    worried about where she will study in secondary
    school.
Of course, I am worried like a beggar who has no
    money, no home and no friends.
You want to ask me if I am worried.
I am worried like a parent because parents want their
    children to study in a good school.
Well, yes, I am worried like a tiger who is worried
    whether it can escape from the cage.
You want to know if I am worried.
I am worried like a poor family which is worried
    because it has no money to buy food.
Well, yes, I am worried like a student who is always
    worried about tests and exams.

Sharon Tang
Primary 6, Heep Yunn Primary School

You wonder if I'm dumb?
OK, then, yes, I'm dumb.

Like a man drinking poison,
watching TV with blind men.

I'm so dumb,
what shall I do?

Cyrus Chan
Form 1, St. Joan of Arc Secondary School

Inside my mother's body
was like sitting on a sofa.
until I grew big.

My mother felt like dying,
until I was born.

Jessica Sze
Form 1, St. Clare's Girls' School

Silly

You wonder if I am silly?
OK, then yes, I am silly.
Like talking to a leaf.
I know it can't hear me
but I'm so silly.

You want to ask, am I silly?
Well, of course, silly.
Like swimming in an empty pool.
I know I can't but
I'm so silly.

If I am silly,
it must be silliness
like putting sugar on sugar-free sweets.

Yes! I'm silly.
Like drinking from an empty bottle.
I know there's nothing,
but I'm so silly.

Don Chan
Form 1, St. Joan of Arc Secondary School

Sad

You ask me if I am sad
Black sad
Sad as black
Black as space
A blackhole with nothing to see
A blackhole that frightens me

Class poem

Depression

You want to know if I'm depressed.
Well, fine, I am, if it makes you content.
Yes, I'm an old woman on a silent road,
my feet bleeding, my knees scraped,
begging on my knees for the mercy of
poverty, the heinous god of misery.
With no pity, he drags me along
the road of misery.

But if I'm depressed,
which I am,
then I can no longer
cry, because I'm an old
towel that has been
wrung many times.

Adrienne Ng
Form 2, Canadian International School

Wine

The blood of a woman
the puke stench,
the caginess of ice,
The toxic taste.

The monster consumes it
greedily
as it staggers in
darkness.

Adrienne Ng
Form 2, Canadian International School

Changed City

A British stood in front of the Legislative Council.
Next to him, not far away,
a Chinese sat beside the national flag,
singing the national anthem.
Well, oh no! All is over.
Anyway, tomorrow will be better.

Fabia Cheng
Form 2, Sacred Heart Canossian College

A Candle

A candle
is a wish from people around,
a sign of love, to celebrate
a marriage.

A candle
is a crisis
a danger of starting a fire
by a little baby.

A candle
is shy little smiling girls
with triangular pink faces.

It's a famous dancer
under the music of winds.
It dances around,
its body is shaking.

A candle
is a tool to forget death.

Anita Mak
Form 2, Sacred Heart Canossian College

Rain

Rain is sharp nails
Dropped onto my skin,
Pointing into my flesh,
Never ending,
Again, again and again.

Rain is a little baby,
Depending on me,
Sleeping on my hand,
sweetly,
comfortably,
never waking up,
never, never.

Kite Kwong
Form 2, Sacred Heart Canossian College

Plain to Fried!

I used to be plain rice,
But now I am fried rice.

I was once white,
But with more friends,
Just like vegetables
Have become colourful
With knowledge and experience,
Just like ham and eggs
Becoming rich.

I used to taste plain,
But with fears, joy, tears,
Just like soy sauce,
Have become tasty –
Sometimes sour,
Sometimes spicy,
Sometimes bitter,
But always sweet.

Yvonne Leung
Form 2, Sacred Heart Canossian College

Constantly Varying

I used to be a cube of ice,
But now I am water,
Melted by the sun.

I used to be water,
But now I am air,
Evaporated.

I used to be a mango,
But now I am a glass of mango juice,
Squeezed in Mary's blender.

I used to be red,
But now I am violet,
Mixed with blue.

I used to be an immaculate white T-shirt,
But now I am a dirty grey T-shirt,
Covered by dust.

I used to be a beauty,
But now I am an ordinary lady,
Getting much older.

I used to be ordinary,
But now I am extraordinary –
I have varied a lot!

Woo Wing Ting, Loretta
Form 2, St. Clare's Girls' School

Hong Kong

Hong Kong, a lazy boy,
always playing with soil,
dirty, dirty and dirty.

Hong Kong, a little baby,
always crying loudly in
the dark,
but no one cares.

Hong Kong, a clock
always talking,
never, never ends.

Hong Kong, a Lego
built to high, high position,
never, never down.

Hong Kong, colour, paint,
with different pictures.

Kite Kwong
Form 2, Sacred Heart Canossian College

Once Upon a Time

Two girls sat in the playground
Eating a loaf of bread.
Wind in September, hot and soft
Like a string joining us closer.
We looked into each other's eyes.
Pointing to the loaf of bread, we said:
'This is our sign'.

I tore a piece of bread and ate it.
It tasted sour and bitter.
The December wind was cruel and sad.
My eyes were full of tears.
No one sat next to me, not even
a little shadow.

Fabia Cheng
Form 2, Sacred Heart Canossian College

Get a Free Balloon!

I
got this
balloon in
Kowloon at noon
If you want to
get a balloon
go there and
get it
As
f
a
s
t
a
s
y
o
u
c
a
n

Kwong Hiu Tong, Karen
Form 2, SKH Bishop Mok Sau Tseng Secondary School

Buddhist

The chanting monks
Each holding a
Beaded necklace
Of praying beads
With each one the same prayer.
All in a repetitive buzz
A bee hive, the air
Thick and dense
With smoke from the
Incense burners.

A bustling palace
Teaming with monks
And believers,
The believers of a king —
Buddha.

I like the chanting
I like the thick air,
All dense with smoke.
I like the hustle and bustle
Because I am
A believer,
I am a Buddhist.

Adrienne Ng
Form 2, Canadian International School

Star

Its bright shining eyes
watch people at night.

People speak to it when they're lonely.
It disappears when the sky cries.

It is always hiding, dancing
on a black stage.

It is too far to reach.

Alice Cheng
Form 2, Sacred Heart Canossian College

Who Am I?

Who am I?
I think I am a bird
flying happily in the sky
smelling fresh air and
touching white clouds.

Who am I?
I think I am a ship
Travelling lonely on the sea
Tasting the sour water and
Facing angry waves.

Who am I?
I think I am a sunflower
Blooming slowly in the garden
Grasping bitter soil and
Receiving acid rain.

Who am I?
I still do not know who I am.

Kite Kwong
Form 2, Sacred Heart Canossian College

When I Grow Up

I don't want to be the Chief Executive,
I'd rather be an ice-cream taster.
And I don't want to be a successful woman,
I'd rather be a crazy woman wandering the streets.
I don't want to be a postman,
I'd rather start a revolution.

Josephine Wong
Form 2, True Light Middle School

Clock

Clock, my mother,
told me the time for study,
the time for eating,
non-rest.

Clock, a baby,
fed by dry cells,
crying everyday,
Ever-lasting.

Clock, the shirts,
Everybody owns them,
Important to you,
Number 1 in your life.

Clock, for one purpose,
born in the factory,
waits in the shop,
homeless.

Clock, an honest girl,
doesn't know how to lie,
shows on the body,
forever humble.

Clock, the bad bacteria,
Shows the deadline,
makes me worry,
makes me nervous.
Finally pains my stomach.

Clock, my MTR,
Rushing to and fro,
Unaffected by accidents,
Non-stop.

Yvonne Leung
Form 2, Sacred Heart Canossian College

Journey

In the village there lies a pond,
And in the pond there is a sky,
And in the sky there hangs a sun.

In the sun there is a fire
That warms the earth and warms the seed,
And in the seed there is a tree.

Within the tree there is a house,
And in that house there lives a boy,
And in the boy there lives adventure.

And in adventure there is a challenge,
And in the challenge there is loss,
And in the loss there is experience.

Cheung Ka Yu
Form 2, Wah Yan College

In the Butterfly There Is a Rainbow

On the leaf there crawls a caterpillar,
In the caterpillar there is a butterfly,
In the butterfly there is a rainbow.

In the rainbow there is an ocean,
In the ocean there is a volcano,
In the volcano, a sea of lava.

In the lava there is a desert,
In the desert there is a fire,
And after the fire a single branch

That points to space,
And in that space there floats a moon,
And in the moon a hare of white,

And in the hare there is a song,
And in that song there is a spell,
And in that spell there is a universe,

A spell of peace,
A spell of happiness,
And from that happiness comes my heart,

And in that heart there floats a moon,
And in the moon there flows an ocean,
And in the ocean a flood of songs,

And in the song there is a hare,
And in the hare there is a fire,
And from that fire a caterpillar crawls.

Lai King Lok
Form 2, Wah Yan College

I Don't Want To Be

When I grow up I don't want to be a dentist,
I'd rather be a panda with a fat body
And sleep and eat every day.
I don't want to be a pharmacist,
I'd rather be a bird with two big wings
Flying in the sky freely.
I don't want to be a banker,
I'd rather be a dog
Walking about with my owner everyday,
No need to worry about anything.
I don't want to be a civil servant,
I'd rather be a CD in a machine
Playing good music.
I don't want to be a student,
I'd rather be a dragon
With powerful head and wings.

Bryan Lie
Form 2, Wah Yan College

Travellers

We have been travelling,
travelling over the
rocks and hills,
travelling over the
seas and plains,
and we have reached
our destination.

We have stayed in our
former destination
and have aged.

We have finished travelling
and we travel once again,
back through the
plains and seas.
We have come back
to our home.

Adrienne Ng
Form 2, Canadian International School

Am I Tense?

Am I tense? Yes, of course, I'm tense.
Like a student waiting for a report card,
or like a speaker forgetting what to say.
I feel like a young woman meeting a handsome man
for the first time.

You want to ask, am I tense?
Of course, aren't I?
Like someone doing an exam.

I'm tense.
Worried and scared.

Fabia Cheng
Form 2, Sacred Heart Canossian College

Jobless Man in Hong Kong

He went into Sogo,
Stared at the clothes.
They're beautiful, aren't they?
He closed his eyes and rushed out.

He followed a crowd into Times Square.
As a lift ascended, men and women
grew smaller.

'Just like my wages, less and less,'
he thought.

Putting his hands in his empty
pockets, he mumbled,
'What can I do?'

Fabia Cheng
Form 2, Sacred Heart Canossian College

Regret

I feel regret
like a person jumping from the building
who can't fly back to the roof.

I am sure I regret
like the ashes of a burned book
which can't be read anymore.

Lau Cho Ying, Candy
Form 3, St. Clare's Girls' School

Abandoned

I remember a day
when my mother left
to visit her mother, sick,
in Australia.
Trembling voice she bid farewell
afraid for our sake.

She left for her plane
to take her far, far away.
My sister, terrified,
six years old
and alone in her world
burst out crying "Mommy!"
My father and I, just four years old,
looked at her strangely and
continued with our computer game.

Stephanie Kwong
Form 3, St. Paul's Convent School

Guilt

You say I'm guilty?
Fine, I'm guilty
as a recepient
at an awards ceremony
stepping on stage
proud
whose sister
gets nothing.

Do I feel guilty?
I do, I do.
Just like a child
stealing candy
without remorse,
yet five years later
feeling the guilt.

Am I guilty?
Sure, I am.
Just like a lawyer
after the verdict
triumphant
while the victim
is crying.

Stephanie Kwong
Form 3, St. Paul's Convent School

Moving Poetry

Why Do I Like Trees?

Because trees smell good
Because trees are tall
Because trees are green and brown and it's a nice
    match
Because trees are quiet
Because I can climb on trees and have fun
Because trees have a longer life than human beings
Grasses always change their mind when the wind
    blows
but trees have a long life.

Chan Miu Ling, Sharon
Form 3, Law Ting Pong Secondary School

Memory

I was young
waiting on London bridge
for the fireworks show.

"Boom" went the fireworks,
lighting up the sky.
The audience exclaimed
"Ooh" and "Ah" everywhere.

There were flowers,
hearts, stars covering
the ceiling.

Sarah Tse
Form 3, True Light Middle School

The Book of Me

How many pages is my imagination?
Only about fifty.
How many pages is my love for my mother?
A little more than a hundred.
How many pages is my love for my father?
A little less than a hundred.
How many pages is my love for my sister?
Approximately seventy-five.
How many pages is my love for the sea?
Two hundred and fifty one.
How many pages is my love for a bowl of noodles?
A dazzling nine hundred.
How many pages is my love for examinations?
Minus twenty one.
How many pages is my love for a street sleeper?
An unreadable fifty two.
How many pages is my love for a rat?
Two.
How many pages is my love for a torn pair of pants?
A surprising seven hundred.
How many pages is my love for a rusted pot?
Five.

Jeffrey Au
Form 3, Canadian International School

Interesting

You think I am interesting?
Surely, I'm interesting –
considered the skinniest in my class,
my friends examine my limbs,
discuss whether they're half
or even one-third their size,
comparing me with a bamboo stick.

Karen Ho
Form 3, St. Paul's Convent School

Yellow

The tiger knocks over the basket.
There are bananas, lemons and mangoes in it.
They all drop on the carpet.
The lion chases after the honeybee.
When I look up,
I see the stars and the moon shining above me.

Cheng Yuk Kin
Form 3, Law Ting Pong Secondary School

Poems by

Teachers

and

Teacher

Apprentices

Extension to the Hong Kong Convention Centre

The figure dips and it sways
It pirouettes then disappears
Behind nooks and crannies
Appearing again in full frontal
It sweeps away
Into a gigantic curve

I follow the flow
Through your bold surfacings
To your most secret interstices
Through your finest mesh
Your exposed girders
I shall remember your multiple nudities
When you become fully drest
As the largest unsupported space in Asia

Louise Ho
from: New Ends Old Beginnings

To a Friend Who Has No Use for Poetry

Yet you remind me of e.e. cummings.

Your desk untidy,
Bills moulded together at the bottom of your wallet,
More sugar please in your already stormy coffee.
To over one hundred people,
You owe at least twenty dollars.

You never read manuals.
Never bother with sunscreen.
Cannonballing off the high board,
Fully dressed,
Tie and all,
Into a pool deep with practicality,
You soak us into smiles.

Timothy Kaiser

An Unexpected Fortune

At the end of the year,
my diary is always very crowded,
two pages of fourteen days or so
marked and crossed all over with
things I must not forget to do,
people I should contact for something,
appointments and meetings for the coming year
bursting through the tiny spaces of the pre-planner.

It is such a pleasure to transfer this mess
into the spacious neatness of a new diary.
Smooth white pages, a full column for each day.
Three hundred and sixty-five of them,
eight thousand, seven hundred and sixty hours in
    total.
Even if I sleep for two thousand, nine hundred and
    twenty hours,
eat away a thousand, bathe and so forth in about five
    hundred,
I shall still have more than four thousand at my
    disposal.

Four thousand hours . . .
Just think of it . . .
A marriage can be consummated in under one.
A friend cheered over the phone in two or three.
Babies born in a matter of ten.
A day trip enjoyed in less than twenty.
A painting completed in perhaps thirty.
A book written in a few hundred . . .

Four thousand clean hours, as yet uncluttered.
So much time, so much life, all for me,
how can I say I am not rich?

A poor woman with an unexpected fortune,
I am determined I shall use it
only for what really matters.

Agnes Lam

Cricket

A cricket flies in through the eleventh floor window
and chirrups to the stand fan as its whirrs,
krik-kik, krik-kik. Bold green and gold against
the ancient brown parquet it waits by its giant
mate, then leaps away when I try to rescue it.
Insect rising to your tiny brain, I open
the balcony doors wide to invite you out
to freedom. But you have hidden under the sofa.

Shirley Geok-lin Lim

The Spotless Dice

Two bony dice polka together
Across the village green of the baize betting table,
Then stopping still, display their spots
Like ladybirds and things of chance.
Dragons of blue smoke hang over them.

Our bride and groom step out again,
Cards turning up in snappy dress and diamonds.
Over the green clearing their scurry, white mice,
Hands swoop over and down on them, white owls,
There is a hooting and screeching above,
The dragons are disturbed and reform lazily.

Dizzy and reckless the gypsy tumblers
Somersault on once more,
Under the bright lights luck and chance
Jostle and trip them.

In the cupboard at night
An old ivory dice big as a ring box tells his tale,
'Somewhere, rolling over the black felt
Of some distant sky is the great spotless dice
Who rolls and rolls and rolls
And never makes a number,
Whose edges have been worn away
Smooth as a billiard ball,
Rolling around in some greater chance,
Free from luck like a holy moon.'

And the dice, with their six flat faces
And their many combinations
Come together, freed for a moment,
Rolling too like holy moons or bladeless stars,
Till one by one, and two by two they tumble
Into a spotless sleep.

Dino Mahoney

Let Us Move

Let us move from lonely to alone
Walk into crowded spaces and be
one of them — any them

Go back to the same place until they expect our face
Salesgirls, bartenders, banktellers
All the public people
counters that tick for anyone everyone

You know the man who runs the corner shop. And the
    guard with no name who
knows you by your floor

Give friendly strangers the liberties you give strange
    friends

From love to rugby to poetry, don't join the club

Don't decide don't divide
Home is where the heart is and the heart is full of
    habit

Hum the schoolsongs that failed to teach you to love
    your country

Pack up your loneliness and shift it from place to
    place

Into the unknown

Voices at the other end of random phone numbers

Leave your eyes on in the dark

Stare back

Sleepwalk

Mani Rao

Afternoon in Cancún

We arrive late. Flamingos walk the inner ring,
marching left. Our money's flat and fits
under the glass, while the woman behind it nods.

Dust is tolerable, almost natural. Rails dangle,
gates built by nuns flake white as possums'
underbellies. Nothing can be said to be clean here,

nothing is lost. Tall, loose as yolks, pink forms
shuffle their mass, stumble on stones, are made to move;
Bountiful, big, brightly made, with a late plumage

of speech, we find the stage. A man with a whip
wrapped around his neck, as though he has nothing
to do with it all, calls, "Birds here."

Page Richards

At the Pier

A fan of fish
swish their fins
under the shadow of
outcrops
gauzed
by hard-boiled seaweeds

The jumbojet
flashes
across the harbour
spraying on my hair
like a veil
smell of salt

My eyes swim
away from the white tail
sinking into the sea

The fish have vanished

Purple casts on the sea surface
flying
like waves

Tsang Chiu Ying, Venus

First Times

The first mouthful of fishball
The joy brought by my first Barbie
The moon rises
The sun sets
My ice-cream weeps

The first lantern on Mid-autumn night
The first packet of Calibee
The wind blows
The typhoon howls
My cotton candy tangles

The first candle on my birthday cake
The first sip of cream soda with milk
The drizzles knit
The rain trickles
My popcorn blossoms

The first sour plum with herbal tea
The first drop of tear down my cheek
Sunrays fade in
Darkness fades out
Times by times add on

Eliza Wong

Our Father

Our Father who art in office,
Hallowed be thy post.
Thy income come,
Thy will be done,
At work but not at home.
Give us this day our daily cash;
And forgive us for ignoring thee,
As we also have forgiven thee for ignoring us;
And lead us not into bankruptcy,
But deliver us from poverty.
For thine is the income, the money and the salary,
For as long as thou art in the labour force –
Poor man.

Wong Ho Yin

Candle

The white candle
flickers
in darkness.

The red candles
at your funeral
sparkled
and looked back
with a smile.

"We acted like candles
in the golden age of journalism. . . ."
The first time I was really
paying attention to a lecturer.

"Be honest about yourself,
be what you really are."
Your words echo.

And you,
who lit my candle
on my graduation
and asked me
to pass it on.
What have I learnt?

Burnt
by the pink little candle
on my first birthday,
I was to face
all these
on my own.

The candle
you hold flames.

Betty Chan

The Case of the SAR

Ladies and Gentlemen:
This is the case of the SAR:
Stranded Ambivalent Race,
Sailing on the Star Ferry,
Halfway across Victoria Harbour,
Between the land of the nine dragons,
And Central, all in five minutes.

French tourists snap pictures,
Balding Chinese men chew on toothpicks,
Screaming children eat fishballs.
Filipino maids chatter,
Tai-tais show off real Gucci bags and Prada shoes.

Sanaz Fotouhi

Despair

One kind of despair,
not my knotted hair
or this under-bridge shelter.
Not these shotgun phrases
I utter, which echo.
Bang. Wham. In retort.
And the gunpowder,
irritation.

Even a princess —
easing on the other side of this wall,
gown of radiating silver
and pink;
ornamented in a dozen exotic blooms,
hair smoothed in golden flecks,
a summer courtyard
warming her cheeks —

is forgotten.
Has she never touched the common?

Cindy Hui

Old Kai Tak

Flicker of shutter blades on this big blackboard
Cuts the murmurs in the hall.
Young wives at the side stare at the slope
Watching for familiar faces.

Children wound with curious energy
Held back yet eager to explore
This beige-brown home of flyers,
Whispering and crying.

Travelers in leisure suits and summer cloth
Carry spices into the melting
Humidity, adding fragrance
And heat to the parade.

We wait for the sound of wheels to fade.

Keon Woong Lee

Food for Thought

Dancing in water,
tail and fins flop,
free at sea.
Until those nets
lurch at it.
That's how we like it.
Fresh, fried, filleted, chopped,
salted, sautéed, served with chips.

The same story unfolds
in Noah's Ark;
chickens, lambs, pigs, cows.
Meat, sanitized, wrapped in plastic
blinds us.

Our stomachs, a graveyard.

Shalini Nanwani

The Day I Turned 18

It is 6 p.m. in Hong Kong on a Thursday
four days after the handover to China. Yes,
it is 1997, and I go for a snack at McDonalds.

I walk down Nathan Road, sun slowly setting,
and eat a hamburger.

I go with my mates to a pub,
alcohol once restricted, but now tasting of
freedom from childhood.

Passing an old man, I sweat, knowing
I am a year closer to my death.

Carl Perito

Snake

Dull brown hid
the gliding animal.
Leathery scales did
Nothing to slow
the rope-like reptile
from where
it was heading.

Moving fast in the fading
grassland, it grazed the ground
without sound.

Raising itself
it hissed and unhinged
its jaws, mouth enlarged
lurching forward to
swallow the creature.

Davina To

Moving Poetry

The Importance of Having an 'R'*

Dea Shopkeepe ,

May I complain about the p inte I bought
at you shop
last week? Today when I am p inting
the manusc ipt of my new play
at home,
I discove the ' ' key is not wo king
at all.

The efo e, I call the publishe
immediately
to cancel the new d ama
tea pa ty.
I tell him the eason,
but he thinks I am making fun
of him.
He asks me which model
I've bought.
It's a mechanical bet ayal
I've caught.

I leave a note at home fo the ca etake ,
telling him he'd bette
not to touch the p inte
in the oom.
But he doesn't know how to ead,
so he asks fo a night out
fo the night school,

---

* The name 'Harold Pinter' (a British dramatist) inspired me to write this
poem. When I looked at the name, I discovered that it looked like the word
'printer' with a missing 'r'. I wondered what would happen to Pinter if one
day he discovered the letter 'r' could not be printed on his printer.

and he claims he will unde stand
my note by the end of next week.

I look fo anothe p inte in the basement,
but the e is none.
So I go out and feed myself
in a café with live band
called No Man's Land.
I am se ved by a dumb waite ,
I o de a c ab f om Alaska,
and she gives me a Baked Alaska,
which is also a kind of Alaska.

I go home with a slight ache
in my stomach,
the neighbou next to my flat
is having a bi thday pa ty.
Noisie than the live band
in No Man's Land,
I just want a piece of silence
fo one night,
so that I can sit down
at my desk and w ite.
But I emembe
I am dep ived of the lette .
I feel like missing a finge .
Gone is the fun of life afte I have lost it.
Finally
I hope you'd unde stand
the impo tance of having an ' '
to me.

You s faithfully
Ha old Pinte

Nicholas Y.B. Wong

Wall

Will you stop looking away
if my eyes accept yours?
You fling your legs lest I sit too close.
Is it because I don't mirror you?

Why should you care if I'm a girl?
I've had enough silence at home,
silence which annoys more when it's broken.

My lovers never call me friend.
Hugs aren't for friends
who tell me their ups and downs,
but not my place in their lives.

Struggling for space
we don't mean to build a wall.

Nicole Wong

Afterword

Poems as Actions: Teaching the Craft of Writing Poems to Hong Kong Schoolchildren

Page Richards

This attempt by all of us to bring children and poems together, it turns out, is like bringing together fish and water. Schoolchildren of Hong Kong already swim. What is a grape for Jessica Sze? "Looks like the earth / Colors the ink of my pen." How does Thomas Chiu see the Peak? Through his father's eyes first: "He said, 'You can see / all the things in Hong Kong.' / I saw many things, more than anyone could see. / I could even see my apartment, / my room, my toys, and my bed."

Moving Poetry started with a voyage by Shirley Geok-lin Lim: to find poems in Hong Kong's children and to revisit Hong Kong through the children's imaginations. As a series of workshops and training sessions in the spring at The University of Hong Kong, Moving Poetry coaxed teachers to hand down the craft of writing poems, a treasure applicable to children everywhere. It is easy for them; they're open to the world. We just help them recognize it.

Learning to be a careful observer is a form of

empathy. It leads to the protection and preservation of the children's home: "Breathe the busy air, feel the excitement, with no pressure," advises Fabia Cheung. At the same time, Hong Kong's international position — its intermingling of tongues — makes words volatile, particularly capable for admitting change and revision. About delivering words to others, Hong Kong poet Leung Ping-kwan writes, "Delivered so, they are no longer the same words; they drift / on an expanse of water, held in the surges and ripples of waves."

Thus, beauty was not only in the children, but in the lesson of developing successful ways to teach the craft of poems in English to Asian schoolchildren. For three Saturdays in late April and early May more than 150 school children in Hong Kong learned how to make things with words. What they created also taught us, the teachers. Any teacher learns from the freshness of children. For Natalie Yeung, just eating a banana lets in the jungle: "When I was eating a banana, a lion roared. / A tiger roared too." And Tsang Hei Man fashions the wind: "I wish I could be the wind. / I wish I could be a wind designer." Yeung Yiu Hong holds down the real: "The sky is blue / When it is / Early morning, / It's yellow orange / In the morning. / It is light blue / In the afternoon." Poems hold up words as choices. The moon creates many moons and a question: "I can see / A red moon / In the morning. / And I can see / A black moon at midnight / Why do I say that?" asks Lee Ka Yee. We are responsible for making those choices increasingly clear and passing on the magic.

All of us teaching for Moving Poetry attempted to do this in our classrooms. It was a big idea, but one that was also in many ways natural, overlooked yet easily available. I have been for years both a teacher and performer. My work on many stages leads me to know that good shows or classes make good participants from their audiences. Thus, the teachers' collaborative work in Moving Poetry leads us, we hope, to join finally with new teachers. The next teachers will help others to recognize and shape patterns of experience, memory for example. A burning candle in the darkened classroom leads Sinting Yip to the memory of a very dark night: "The stars still sparked, but not as bright as before." Then begins a second memory of dreams: "The scene led me back to my dreams."

Both private journal and public document, our classrooms included Main Building 201, Seminar Room 113G, and the large conference room by the courtyard, Room 104. Private conversations between teachers and students began about sharks' wetness and bears' loudness, the subjects. Experienced teachers interrupted Chau Ton and Hiu Laam to help. The shark's wetness becomes cleanliness: "What's your body when it's wet?" / Can you make it clean?" The bear too was refashioned in private, back at the desk. "Shouting loud," the bear is asked, "What happened to you?"

Compiling a public record of successful practices started as soon as we spoke together about our ideas. Shirley Geok-lin Lim and I began by leading training sessions for the teacher-poets in the Main Building to outline together some of these exercises. We all agreed, for instance, upon a circle formation for the chairs, rather than lines. In a circle the children would feel part of one another. (The circle remained the metaphor; each class we came 'round and 'round to the same patterns but with more to think about, more to feel.) Animal poems were suggested as inviting themes. We also talked about activities in which the whole of the children's bodies would be involved: noses, fingers, ears, hands. One teacher developed an extraordinary exercise using perspective. As the teacher said, this approach was inspired by Wallace Stevens's poem "Thirteen Ways of Looking at a Blackbird," in which a blackbird, flying out of sight, "marked the edge / Of one of many circles." Made of words, the children's poems also came out of seeing an object *relationally*. Each child was asked to stand near an object, such as a candle, then walk far away from it and look back. A student could also hold the same object above the head, just before standing on a desk to look down on it. One girl saw a candle's action by creating a second look. The flame is first a "crisis." Then this: "A candle / is shy little smiling girls / with their triangular, pink faces."

We talked together about adding music, such as Pachelbel, to aid memory. In class, the exercise was turned into a home for memory. Pachelbel was played, while the sound of waves was added. The children were still, as they remembered something. Immediately paper was handed out, and the children wrote about their experiences of things or people in Hong Kong: "Mr. Lai took me / to ride on the Star Ferry," began Helen Lai. Feeling seasick but special, the rider concludes, "Why couldn't the sea / not have any waves? / But the waves are / beautiful."

Varying tone and timing was also important for us. We discussed having them work independently, and in groups. One teacher's exercise had each child contribute one line to a class pastiche: "My legs are as long as snakes. / The turtles are as hard as titanium. / Lions sound like my school bell. / . . . My eyes are fishballs, when I was a baby," begins one collaborative poem. While the students were working, we agreed, we would generally let them forget about punctuation and spelling and grammar. As one teacher said, "Grammar and sense should not be over-emphasized if we want to enter their poetic world." We encouraged the reading of poems out loud to one another, including group readings. Recitations of the city names, for example — Shanghai, Seattle, Toronto, Beijing — permitted us to be born again, together as poets.

Language for poems is also action, a way children can move themselves from one place to another: from a "before" to an "after," from being small to being big, from the body of a person to the mind of an animal (we had given the smallest children beanie babies, so each child had an immediate friend from another world). We wanted poems as transportation from one world to another, from a "soft patch of grass" to a plane over Phuket, from Pokfulam Road to the inside of Carol Yu's tick of time: "The plant of life nourishes on something / called time, / from which days, hours and minutes pass by / all started in the tick of a second." Out of the tick comes something special: "The hours extend into the brilliant sunset, / and from it blossoms the night sky, / and within the night lies twinkles of sprinkling."

Poems were a way to move them into new ways of themselves. Some students at first were afraid: what to do with this unusual thing in their hands? One girl had written a shape poem, in the form of a balloon, but did not trust its *poemness*. Her teacher had to slide the paper gently but forcefully from the top of her desk to collect it. Older students occasionally felt self-conscious. Poems belonged to poets they had studied: Li Po and Shakespeare and Meng Hao-jan. How could they, young people sitting near the main courtyard one afternoon, compete? But listen to Jenny Cheng: "I wish I were a map holding the ocean and land."

We are aware, too, that poems have too often been painfully reduced to "meanings" or "messages." Poems are not that. All of us look at them as a way *to see* or — better — as a way *to move*. As poems move forward, so does a student's self-confidence. By choosing "a goose" instead of "a bird," for example, a miracle happens. The long "o" is funny. A long neck appears with it. A goose lives in places that ostriches, for instance, don't inhabit. So a world appears around the goose that was not there before. "Goose" also has associations with fairy tales and golden eggs. When Justin Ching Ho, a boy who had been given a goose beanie baby, chose the word "goose" in his poem for "bird," he saw an abyss and a dive and something else, the beauty and horror of its mechanics: "Among the creatures of the deep, / I saw a goose, / in metallic grey, / diving in the abyss, / stealthily, neck straight." In other words, he thought in new ways by saying in new ways. By seeing the goose slowly he saw its metallic feathers. Sight and insight combine, and Justin becomes both a witness and a creator.

What worked best in our classrooms occurred when children perceived and wrote images simultaneously in sounds, touch, and action. One of the teachers had the lights turned out while the children passed around several objects to taste, smell, touch, and hear. Anita Mak knows a pineapple: "Hard and dry outside, / Green hat on head." I had them paint a house (it could be anything, a horse or person) twice. The first time, they were asked to give exceedingly little detail. The second time they were to see the same image in slower motion. We also tried sometimes to slow their hands down. Some of them painted in slow motion as well. Every body part is a part of the whole, so the organ of the eye is slowed down appreciably after the children learn to slow their hands in painting. By using their fingers to paint and immediately moving their fingers to write, they found shaping to be alike in both drawing and writing. In the first picture, Stephanie Tsang's house had a path; in the second, it was red with "clear" windows and "green bushes," and — surprise! — "juicy red strawberries around it."

Teachers regularly went around the room to hear all the voices. One boy was immediately engaged by the attention. He was lovely, thick-haired, very formally dressed. Serious, he was a reminder of Coventry Patmore's exquisite "Son," with the careful and serious play of a child: "My little Son, who look'd from thoughtful eyes / And moved and spoke in quiet grown-up wise . . . had put within his reach, / A box of counters and a red-vein'd stone / A piece of glass abraded by the beach . . . And two French copper coins, ranged there with careful / art, / To comfort his sad heart." The children did not consider carefulness to be an unnatural addition to language-making.

Our assistants helped to make the settings, as much as possible, playful, open, inviting. We did not stand in the center of the circle. We all walked around and made suggestions for a poem that might be a special fit: a boy's cap, a girl's blue-striped pen. Assistants often began at the other end of the circle so that the attention was immediately forthcoming. Children raised their hands, thrust their papers forward for us to see. Some of the boys called out the parts of their poems that required help. As one teacher said, "kids found it really hard to express a feeling that they had not thought about; they really needed us to provide materials for them as we asked them to think, transform, and create out of the given materials."

Children need some kind of form to begin. The language for poems can be found in the most common things, such as paint. Children can learn ways to thin language (when it needs more light), to add blues and greens and black (when contrast is important), to move it with a brush in stanzas of three lines, four lines, short lines, half lines. Teachers can help them. Kenneth Koch, a poet who has worked extensively with teaching the craft of poems in New York to children and to whom this project is indebted, has found several examples of actions that help to organize perceptions: "I Used To/ But Now"; "I Seem To Be/ But Really I Am," both of course variations on "Before/After." With help from poets such as Adrienne Rich and Langston Hughes, we added some: "You're wondering if I'm *lonely*: / OK then, yes, I'm *lonely*" and "I've known *rivers*: / Ancient, dusky *rivers*," for example. Other exercises included fairy tales: one class reimagined the fairy-tale structure for modern Hong Kong stories: "Cinderella went to the fireworks all fancy," begins Becky Martyn. Whom does she meet? "Cinderella went to the fireworks. / She met a business tycoon." Another class asked about trees: "Why Do I Like Trees?" "Because trees are tall. Trees are strong. / They aren't afraid of the rain and storm," answers Ng

Chung Yan. Color poems came out of one class. About Yellow, there were tigers knocking over baskets with "bananas, lemons, and mangoes in it," witnessed by Cheng Yuk Kin.

Deliberately, we sometimes made famous, well-crafted poems worse. We did it to show them what was lost. We reduced a runner in a Walt Whitman poem to statement: "There is a runner on the street . . . . He runs with his arms at his side." We had them stand up and imitate such a runner. Then we had them imitate *the* runner, Whitman's runner with his "lightly closed fists." They saw more. They felt their own bodies more delicately. One boy, Xavier Tam, chose a slam dunk and saw it more keenly, connected it to other things he has thought about: a skunk's "heart is a basketball that is dribbled by a player left and right." We hoped that they would see such comparisons, comparisons that later will turn into histories for them, the beauty of histories in expression: eventually, *shan-sui-shih*, Chinese poems of "mountains and rivers," ballads, sonnets, yes, but also pediments and fugues and, when they're older perhaps, cycles of history and families.

Part of our responsibility was to create such background maps and continuities, ones they could inhabit and write and revise for themselves. One method was to create links and repetitions through all the sessions. A class, for instance, had four parts each session: the "stimulus" stage; writing stage; recitation stage; finalizing of drafts for submission. Another worked consistently with haiku. In two of our classes, we entered the lives of animals progressively. William Blake's poem, "The Tyger," beginning, "Tyger! Tyger! burning bright / In the forests of the night," led the way in one class. June Lau, rethinking her pony, responded, "If you hear me, neigh, neigh / You know I am trotting by / like the wind, the wind." In another, the children wrote the names of their beanie babies on the board, along with the kind of animal, its habitat, how it moves, what it does in the day, what it does at night. Each week, of course, the board was erased. Each week they started again. They could write what they wrote before *or* revise what they wrote by adding detail, following the "life" of the animal more closely, now that they were learning to see in slow motion.

Increasingly, they entered the mind of the animal that they originally were only writing *about*. At first they did not see this, but the elements on the board every week become more accurate, more precise in vision and attention. Where there was a rabbit on the board, there soon appears a "nibbler." That same "nibbler" by the third class, on the board, becomes a "nibbler nibbling leaves."

Children liked writing on the board, and they were at the same time transgressing. They dared at the board, and they brought that important, wonderful feeling back with them to their desks. Like the haiku and like the four-part sessions, the repetition of the practice became refrains that we made for them. Like a good refrain the pattern began to fold into the children's poems. We therefore tried to have the children recycle what they learned and increase their abilities. We all taught revision regularly, at first in literal ways: seeing things again. A scientist in a first drawing stands nowhere in particular; in the second the scientist has experiments in a lab, so the verb changed from "thinks" to "experiments."

Revisions could be difficult, however. For a flower, they tried "tulip," then "blank tulip." A "line of birds" became "birds flying in a line." For verbs, some looked again at their pictures. Poems are made out of words, not ideas first. Some were not afraid at all. They allowed words their multiple lives. Words, like children, have many lives, and children can intuitively free words from a single restrictive meaning or use. Indeed, we recognized one thing that the bilingual ear offers: an ability to hear words easily as sounds. The students moved to accommodate possible shapes of words, disconnected from a single meaning or association. For instance, when a man in a poem moved "hummingly," they already remembered the word *in relation* to other words by sound: "stunning," "strumming." The adverbial "ly" function, therefore, was for them the smaller sound. One natural action of a poem, seeing something in relation to something else — as *like* — is built into multiple tongues. Hearing patterns of sound, and deriving pleasure from that, has natural footing.

In addition to being quiet, through sounds such as "hummingly," poetry is noisy: "So, I like evening very much. / Why? Why? Why? / It's because the sun and the sky / Are orange in the evening," explains Yim Man Kit. It is conversational, as well as elusive and suggestive. It talks across generations even before it utters its first word. We continued to teach the children forms: repetition, comparison, refrains. The patterns behind these forms are not unique to poems. They are the patterns of generations, of reproduction, of being "like" and "unlike." They are patterns of return.

But how do children learn to hear how exactly poetry is social, how it speaks to the living, the dead, ancestors, friends, old kings and queens, dragons, and a nearby azalea rooting itself to Bonham Road? How do these same children learn not to associate it either with a purely private language or a social mask? How? Children, like poems, are naturally noisy as well as quiet, conversational as well as enigmatic. Children are naturally social in the ways that poems are naturally private, and vice versa. That is, they instinctively resort to ceremony as a way to express themselves privately and intimately with parents, family, and friends. Therefore, they talk to other children less often by statement than by gesture: both hands and feet drooping, smiles half-made or unreturned. Long before words, these gestures clue children in to other children and their surroundings and to themselves again.

So poems follow the same circles. They talk to one another across centuries in sonnets, wave open arms in free verse, have controlled conversations to one another in syllabics. And in so doing they understand their own social *and* private worlds better. Rita Dove, an African-American poet teaching at the University of Virginia, holds a conversation with William Blake, a White Englishman of the eighteenth century; reinventing his patterns, she finds her own voice and surroundings nearer: "Sometimes there were things to watch — / the pinched armor of a vanished cricket, a floating maple leaf. . . ." Just as poems invent one another, so do children. The form of poems is the first subject of the poem. A noted reader of poems, Helen Vendler, points to possible acts: "Is [the] poem a Boast, or an Apology, or a Prayer?" The actions of children, too, take place in words, and they can recognize in ceremony a private feeling. The movement of a polar bear is dance, and its beauty is transformative, generational, for its watcher: "A polar bear / With a thick white coat / Walking in the strong wind / Stepping on the cold ice . . . It will never rest / Till it finds the food / For its lovely baby."

Children want to express themselves more clearly and by doing so know themselves better. Whether or not the children continue to write poems, we hoped each of them felt a new kind of attention (more close and more slow) inside their bodies. We think some of them did feel this already. Kite Kwong watched the rain: "Rain is a little baby, depending on me." Tsang Hei Man is aware of an owl: "I have an owl / Called John." He pays attention to its night habits: "It always flies / In my bedroom / and eats the flowers." Hong Kong, under Yvonne Leung's watch, grows: "One tiny dot, / With all combines, / With all amazes." The students moved through poems and they were moved by poems. The children moved us with their eagerness, fears and skillful recoveries, their openness.

Soon their words, when you see them on buses and subways and posters, will move you too. Their words will take you back home — to Hong Kong — in a way you've never felt before. Hong Kong has fantastic rains and flowers, and pineapples and "busy air." One teacher said the children's "joy and gaiety" made her "see [her] world differently." We have seen it better because of the children who came and let us know their words. They, and we through them, revisit what Ng Cho calls "a wonderful place," Mong Kok, and the larger Hong Kong.